GREAT MOVIE
Instrumental Solos

D1385387

Alfred

Alfred Music
P.O. Box 10003
Van Nuys, CA 91410-0003
alfred.com

ISBN-10: 0-7390-4367-6
ISBN-13: 978-0-7390-4367-7

BATTLE OF THE HEROES

(From *Star Wars*®: Episode III *Revenge of the Sith*)

Music by
JOHN WILLIAMS

Maestoso, with great force (♩ = 92)

Battle of the Heroes - 2 - 1
26222

DOUBLE TROUBLE

(From Warner Bros. Pictures'
HARRY POTTER AND THE PRISONER OF AZKABAN)

Medieval in spirit (♩ = 92)

Music by
JOHN WILLIAMS

26222

STAR WARS

(Main Title)

(From *Star Wars*®: Episode III *Revenge of the Sith*)

Music by
JOHN WILLIAMS

SUPERMAN THEME

Music by
JOHN WILLIAMS

Superman Theme - 2 - 1
26222

RAIDERS MARCH

Music by
JOHN WILLIAMS

Raiders March - 2 - 1
26222

HOGWARTS' HYMN

(From Warner Bros. Pictures'
HARRY POTTER AND THE GOBLET OF FIRE)

By PATRICK DOYLE

WONKA'S WELCOME SONG

Music by DANNY ELFMAN

(À la yodel)

THE IMPERIAL MARCH
(Darth Vader's Theme)

Music by
JOHN WILLIAMS

THE NOTEBOOK
(Main Title)

By AARON ZIGMAN

Slowly, with expression (♩ = 69)

26222

INTO THE WEST

Words and Music by
FRAN WALSH, HOWARD SHORE,
ANNIE LENNOX

Into the West - 2 - 1
26222

PARTS OF A FLUTE AND FINGERING CHART

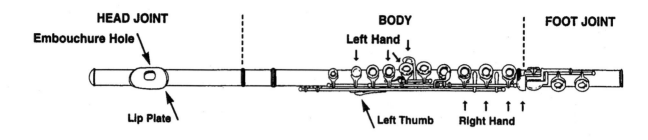

HEAD JOINT **BODY** **FOOT JOINT**

Embouchure Hole

Left Hand

Lip Plate

Left Thumb   Right Hand

● = press the key.
○ = do not press the key.

When there are two fingerings given for a note, use the first one unless the alternate fingering is suggested.

When two enharmonic notes are given together (F♯ and G♭ as an example), they sound the same pitch and played the same way.